REYKJAVÍK

CITY GUIDE *for* DESIGN LOVERS

The Travel Colours City Guides are for design-loving travellers who like to explore the trendiest places in each city, for travellers who see themselves as trendsetters. Each City Guide features a curated selection of the best places to "sleep, eat, drink, shop and explore", all of which have been personally tried and tested.

Edition ONE | 2019

EDITOR IN CHIEF
STEFANIE FRIESE

PHOTOGRAPHY BY
FLAVIA RENZ

WORDS BY
HANNI HEINRICH, STEFANIE FRIESE

COVER DESIGN BY
NAROSKA DESIGN, BERLIN

PUBLISHED BY
FRIESE MEDIA GMBH, 2018
1ST EDITION - DECEMBER 2018
PRINTED AND BOUND IN GERMANY ON
FSC CERTIFIED UNCOATED PAPER

ISBN 978-3-9819822-6-8

SAY HELLO

GENERAL ENQUIRIES: hello@travelcolours.de
DISTRIBUTION: sales@travelcolours.de

GET THE BOOKS ONLINE AT
www.travelcolours.de

WE TAKE CARE

OF YOU AND OF MOTHER EARTH

Our books are printed exclusively on FSC-certified paper. FSC certification indicates that the wood fibers come from a forest that is managed responsibly. The wood is harvested in such a way that any negative impact on the environment is greatly reduced.

Our commitment goes even further. We work closely with a family-run printing company that has been printing climate-neutral for years together with ClimatePartner. Only organic inks are used for printing, and these are readily biodegradable and free of toxic ingredients. Neither water nor chemicals are needed for our exposure process.

STEFANIE FRIESE

It has to be nice and a bit different. The desire for lifestyle and design is always guaranteed. As the founder of Travel Colours, Stefanie travels the world in search of the most beautiful places to sleep, eat, drink, shop and explore.

FLAVIA RENZ

Being based in Berlin, Flavia loves to keep herself surrounded by all that is beautiful and yummy. Camera in hands, you usually find her standing on any furniture available, just to get that picture framed perfectly.

HANNI HEINRICH

As a writer, Hanni is inspired by people, human behaviour and beaches. Her favourite body lotion is sun blocker factor 50. Born in Merseburg, Germany, she is currently based in Cape Town.

LOVE LETTER

Everyone has heard of Iceland's dramatic nature - glaciers right next to active volcanoes, bubbling geysers and hot springs, black lava beaches and the graceful dancing Northern Lights every visitor secretly hopes to see.
With the dramatic rise of tourism, Iceland has quietly gained a worldwide reputation for its surprisingly dynamic food scene. Foodies in Reykjavík will find plenty of restaurants serving traditional ingredients in a creative, new way. While Iceland used to be a seemingly remote island of isolation, it has turned into an international hot spot. If you're planning on spending time in Reykjavík, you'll be easily seduced by its exciting food and drink scene, Nordic architecture and the pop art scene, as well as the vibrant nightlife that shows how different this city is to anywhere else in the world.
From local coffee roasters and Iceland's first Michelin-star restaurant, to iconic fashion and design companies, this guide will show you a curated selection of our favourite places to "sleep, eat, drink, shop and explore" in Reykjavík - the world's most northerly capital.

Stefanie Friese

EDITOR IN CHIEF

SLEEP

ION CITY HOTEL

COOL NORDIC DESIGN

People say this is the hippest hotel in Reykjavík. The architecture resembles Iceland's nature. The lobby imitates nature with a real birch tree behind the reception desk and a "bird's nest" light hanging from the ceiling. Hallways and other rooms are more modern and futuristic, but the mood and atmosphere are all about Scandi-style comfort with a hint of coziness provided by wooden wall panels. The rooms all offer modern amenities with anti-allergy bedding. All bedroom doors have a sound isolation of 45db. A good night's sleep is guaranteed as Reykjavík's nightlife goes on buzzing.

Laugavegur 28, 101 Reykjavík
www.ioniceland.is

SKUGGI HOTEL

STYLISH ROOMS IN THE CENTRE

Timeless, modest and clear-cut design reflects the style of this hotel. Centrally located in downtown Reykjavík, Skuggi Hotel is a great base from which to explore the city. The hotel has a total of 100 rooms, all of which are tastefully decorated in a consistent style. The black-volcanic-gray aesthetic can be found in the lobby, the hotel bar and is carried through to the rooms. The inspiration for the interior comes from photographs of Icelandic nature by Ragnar Axelsson which, mixed with city charm, create a raw but cozy atmosphere. Above the beds in each room is a reference from Ragnar's book, Behind the Mountains.

Hverfisgata 103, 101 Reykjavík
www.keahotels.is/en/hotels/skuggi-hotel

EXETER HOTEL

CONTEMPORARY DESIGN HOTEL

Staying in a historical building from 1904 close to Reykjavík's old harbour offers a great local experience with all the perks of a designer hotel. The main building is a restoration and linked to newer and more modern buildings. Exeter Hotel is a tribute to both contemporary architecture and traditional Icelandic fishing times. Sauna and fitness rooms are accessible to guests. The 106 rooms are equipped with modern amenities in an industrial yet elegant Nordic style. The restaurant and in-house bakery offer honest home-made food and local delicacies like Icelandic potato bread.

Tryggvagata 12, 101 Reykjavík
www.keahotels.is/en/hotels/exeter-hotel

EXETER HOTEL

KEX HOSTEL

HOUSED IN AN OLD BISCUIT FACTORY

Once this hostel was a soulless building belonging to an old biscuit factory. Now the Kex Hostel is a social place in downtown Reykjavík, just a few steps from the sea. It sleeps 215 people with a variety of dorms and rooms, along with a restaurant, bar, lounge area, heated outdoor patio, old school gym, guest kitchens, and a multifunctional hall called Gym & Tonic. The vintage yet hip modern flair still reminds one of the old factory: Kex is the Icelandic word for biscuit. Locals enjoy the great cuisine at Kex because it invites everyone to feel at home.

Skúlagata 28, 101 Reykjavík
www.kexhostel.is

THE WORLD
HEMISPHERES

CANOPY BY HILTON REYKJAVÍK

SIX HISTORICAL HOUSES

The Canopy by Hilton hotel is located on Hverfisgata Street in the city centre just a few minutes' walk from the harbour, where whale-watching tours and boat trips depart. Comprising six historical houses that were once part of a furniture factory, Canopy is the first hotel in the Hilton group's new self-billed "lifestyle hotel" brand. The hotel is designed to feel and breathe Reykjavík's cool factor. The 112 rooms and suites are individually decorated. The interiors reflect calming Icelandic colour schemes of ocean, ice and volcanic rock. Every detail inside is meticulously thought out and beautifully crafted to feel homely while also making a design statement.

Smidjustigur 4, 101 Reykjavík
www.canopy3.hilton.com

SAND HOTEL

MODERN DESIGN MEETS RICH HERITAGE

Wake up to smell of freshly baked bread! This is possible at this new four-star boutique hotel in the heart of downtown Reykjavík. Its location on Lagavegur makes it a desirable place to stay, with bustling city life and rich culture just around the corner.

All rooms are decorated in a cozy art deco style. Original contemporary artwork makes each room individual, while the warm colour palette combined with comfortable upholstered furniture, curtains and other soft materials gives the rooms a relaxed atmosphere and boutique feeling. On the ground floor of the hotel are the Sandholt Bakery and Guðsteins Eyjólfssonar haberdashery, both of which have been in continuous business for over 100 years.

Laugavegur 34, 101 Reykjavík
www.keahotels.is/en/hotels/sand-hotel

RECEPTION

APOTEK HOTEL

SET IN A HISTORICAL BUILDING

The Apotek Hotel is housed in one of the oldest and most beloved buildings dating from 1917, the Reykjavík Apothecary. Today, the historic pharmacy is a five-star hotel and welcomes guests with a blend of comfortable modern design and accents of the past that celebrate the rich history of the building. The Apotek Hotel features 45 luxurious rooms - all of them with a modern look mixed with a classic touch to match the hotel's exterior and fully equipped with modern amenities.

The building was built by the state architect and visionary Guðjón Samúelsson, who at the time was the most commissioned architect in Iceland. Some of his numerous buildings include the Hallgrimskirkja, the National Theater of Iceland and the sister hotel, Hotel Borg.

Austurstræti 16, 101 Reykjavík
www.keahotels.is/en/hotels/apotek-hotel

EAT

WITH COFFEE

BRAUÐ & CO

ARTISANAL BAKING

Organic and inspired by tradition and simplicity. Located in the heart of Reykjavík, Brauð & Co is a small local bakery focusing on high quality local ingredients and honesty. Real hands bake real bread behind an open glass kitchen, so guests and pedestrians can watch the process. One can also talk to the bakers and ask questions about the ingredients. No fancy food decoration, no additives. Brauð & Co is pure and beautiful. This makes every single bun in this bakery unique. From croissants, bread loaves and nutty and fruity bread rolls to traditional Icelandic bread delicacies, every individual taste will be satisfied here. Brauð & Co has other bakeries in Reykjavík, each with its own individual charm.

www.braudogco.is

STOFAN

CAFÉ WITH A RELAXED ATMOSPHERE

Stofan is a cozy cafe in the heart of Reykjavík at Ingólfstorg Square. It offers coffee specialities, a selection of Icelandic beers, wines, home-made cakes, bagels and whiskeys. Those who prefer savoury bites will also find happiness at Stofan. Stofan is Icelandic for living room, and that's exactly what it feels like: vintage sofa chairs, wooden tables, mismatched mugs, warm lighting, boardgames to play, books to read and, an added bonus, free high-speed Wi-Fi. Business meetings are held here and digital nomads work here. It is easy to spend the entire afternoon at Stofan.

Aðalstræti, 101 Reykjavík
www.facebook.com/stofan.cafe/

2. Præmie
Cup Tasters DM 2012
1.
Præmie
Barista
DM 2012
FLEETWOOD MAC

REYKJAVÍK ROASTERS

FOR SERIOUS COFFEE DRINKERS

This roastery will please everyone who is looking for the best full-bodied, versatile coffee in town. The concept behind the company is simple: good beans, roasted with care and brewed to the best. With three locations in Iceland's capital, Reykjavík Roasters uses fair coffee produced with full respect for both human beings and nature. The beans are carefully selected from Brazil to Ethiopia, with an ever-new, interesting batch to try out. The newest café opened in late September 2018 on the first floor of Ásmundarsalur. The house was built in 1934 and was once home to sculptor Ásmundur Sveinsson. Today it serves as a gallery and makes an enjoyable space for all art lovers who enter the café.

www.reykjavikroasters.is

GOTT

HEALTHY AND FLAVOURFUL FOOD

There are many ways to find one's self and one's home while traveling. Sigurður Gíslason and his wife, Berglind Sigmarsdóttir, found each other after having worked everywhere in the world, from the Bahamas to New York. Now the couple's home is Gott in Iceland, a healthy, creative restaurant with roots in Vestmannaeyjar. Fresh, authentic ingredients is the focus. All sauces, broths, soups, bread and cake are handmade in the restaurant and fresh fish from the market is brought in every morning. The interior is playful and luxury at the same time and often matches the colours of the food. The two owners have also published two best-selling cookery books in Iceland and one in Germany.

Hafnarstræti 17, 101 Reykjavík
www.facebook.com/GottReykjavik

LE KOCK 2.0 - TAIL

STREET FOOD BY PROFESSIONAL CHEFS

Three men, one diner! Located downtown in the ground floor of the Exeter Hotel, this street food restaurant is run by three professional chefs who love honest food including what may be the best burgers in Iceland: classic burgers, fish and chips made with Icelandic potatoes, spring onion salad and home-made doughnuts. The portions are generous, as men know what it means to put hardware on the plate. Karl is responsible for drinks and enjoys collecting beers and wines. Markús is the „chef turned baker" who makes sure the associated bakery rides the waves smoothly and Knútur defines the term organized chaos.

Tryggvagata 14, 101 Reykjavík
www.lekock.is

GR A
N D I
MATHÖLL
GRANDI MATHÖLL
MATHÖLL

GRANDI MATHÖLL

FOOD HALL IN THE GRANDI HARBOUR DISTRICT

How does one explore Iceland's food, culture and social life in only one day? At Grandi Mathöll. Nestled in the Grandi harbour district, this food hall is part of the most innovative area in Reykjavík. Housed in a refurbished fish factory, Grandi Mathöll is a heavenly and obvious destination for anyone who loves to explore delicious food, quality products and culture. Stools, benches and couches scattered throughout the spaces provide comfort and allow one to relax while enjoying different types of foods. People meander between Asian vendors and 9 artisanal street food stands offering Icelandic fish and meat. Fresh Icelandic vegetables, freshly brewed coffee and other drinks are also available.

Grandagarður 16, 101 Reykjavík
www.grandimatholl.is

THE COOCOO'S NEST

NESTLED IN AN OLD FISHING HUT

This vibrant nest is located just a tad further out from the old harbour. The Coocoo's Nest offers brunch, delicatessen items and dinners. Each day the menu varies, from "Taco Tuesday" to "Sourdough Pizza" evenings or "Natural Wine" days. Gourmets will be spoiled as dishes like ocean perch crudo with fermented watermelon, pickled mustard seeds and Icelandic kombu, open vegan falafel sandwiches with baba ganoush and jalapeño cashew aioli & celery root coleslaw will be presented in the most stylish way, each screaming for an Oscar. From soup to salads to aperitivos and main courses, The Coocoo's Nest offers it all. Come early as no reservations are taken!

Grandagarður 23, 101 Reykjavík
www.coocoosnest.is

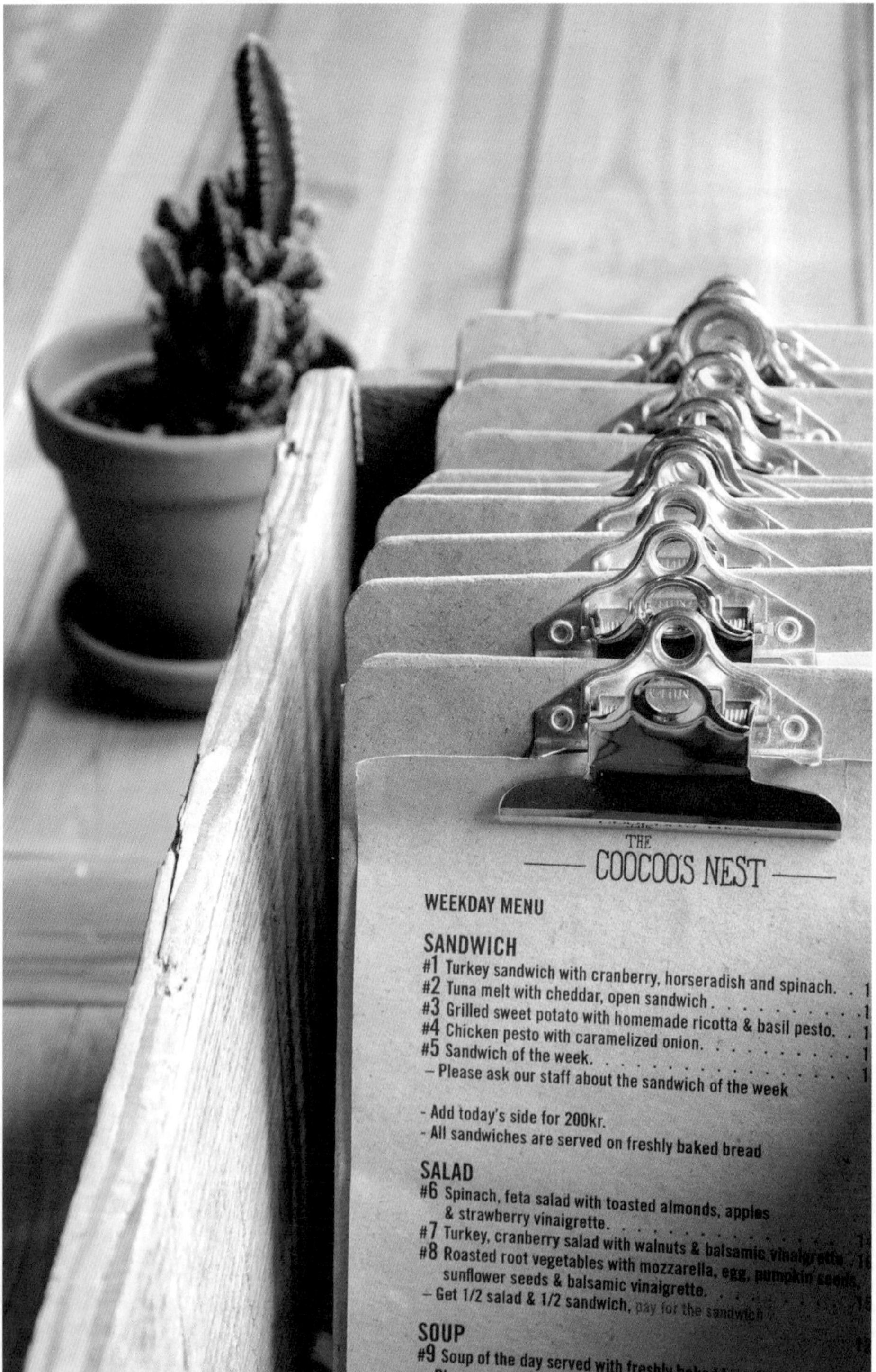
THE
COOCOO'S NEST
WEEKDAY MENU
SANDWICH
#1 Turkey sandwich with cranberry, horseradish and spinach.
#2 Tuna melt with cheddar, open sandwich
#3 Grilled sweet potato with homemade ricotta & basil pesto.
#4 Chicken pesto with caramelized onion.
#5 Sandwich of the week.
– Please ask our staff about the sandwich of the week
- Add today's side for 200kr.
- All sandwiches are served on freshly baked bread
SALAD
#6 Spinach, feta salad with toasted almonds, apples
& strawberry vinaigrette.
#7 Turkey, cranberry salad with walnuts & balsamic vinaigrette
#8 Roasted root vegetables with mozzarella, egg, pumpkin seeds,
sunflower seeds & balsamic vinaigrette.
– Get 1/2 salad & 1/2 sandwich, pay for the sandwich
SOUP
#9 Soup of the day served with freshly baked bread
– Please ask our staff

KAFFIVAGNINN
FRESH FISH
ALL DAY
FISH
& CHIPS

KAFFIVAGNINN

ICELAND'S OLDEST RESTAURANT

Located in the old harbour district, this eatery offers comfort food the way grandmother made it. The windows in this restaurant are so wide, bobbing boats can be seen while having brunch or a hearty seafood lunch. Kaffivagninn has been popular since 1935. It is the oldest operating restaurant in the country, no less. The name translates to "The Coffee Wagon," and the restaurant was a literal wagon to begin with. The menu has stayed down to earth and true to the people who frequent it. Seafood and smørrebrød, breakfast and brunch, pancakes and pies: simply does it.

Grandagarður 10, 101 Reykjavík
www.kaffivagninn.is

KAFFIVAGNINN

RBRA

BERGSSON MATHÚS

FRIENDS OF VEGETARIANS AND VEGANS

Fresh, healthy and cozy, Bergsson Mathús puts great emphasis on first-class ingredients, be it for breakfast, lunch or dinner, all served in a relaxing atmosphere. Bergsson Mathús are friends of vegetarian and vegan food. Since its opening, the café has been a popular meeting place for locals interested in food. Despite the compact menu, the choices for vegetarians and vegans vary widely. From free-range eggs and greenhouse-grown vegetables to sourdough bread with Icelandic butter and home-made compotes. Colourful magazines and newspapers are on the tables, and the picturesque Reykjavík "Pond", popular for feeding duck, is just a stone's throw away.

Templarasund 3, 101 Reykjavík
www.bergsson.is

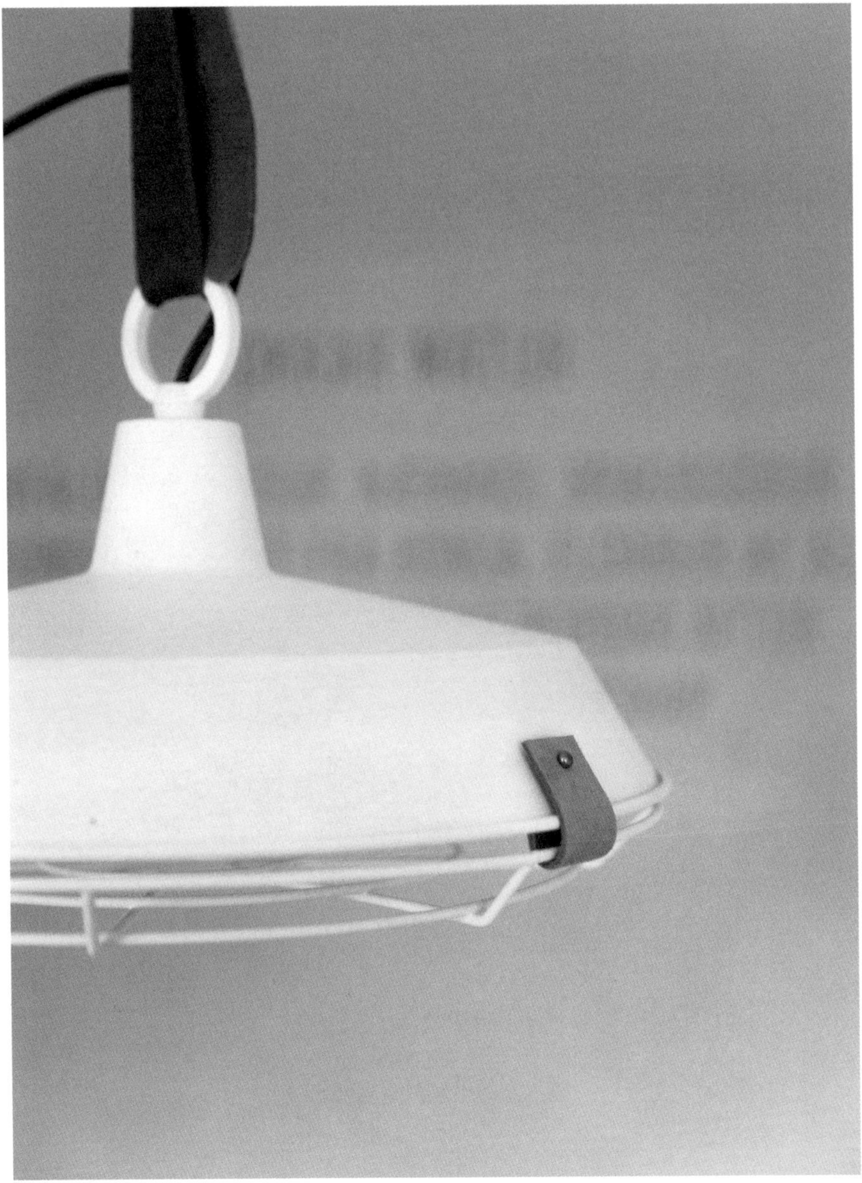

BÆJARINS BEZTU PYLSUR

BEST HOT DOG STAND IN EUROPE

Where is the world's most famous hot dog stand located? In the heart of Reykjavík! Bæjarins Beztu Pylsur, which means the best hot dog in town, is literally the most popular hot dog stand in central Reykjavík. Not only have the majority of Icelanders eaten here, but also famous people including former US President Bill Clinton and James Hetfield, the Metallica vocalist. In August 2006, the newspaper The Guardian selected Bæjarins Beztu as the best hot dog stand in Europe and it reached global fame. This business also has a long tradition: since 1937 Bæjarins Beztu has been located in the Reykjavík's harbour and has become a true Icelandic institution.

Tryggvagata 1, 101 Reykjavík
www.bbp.is

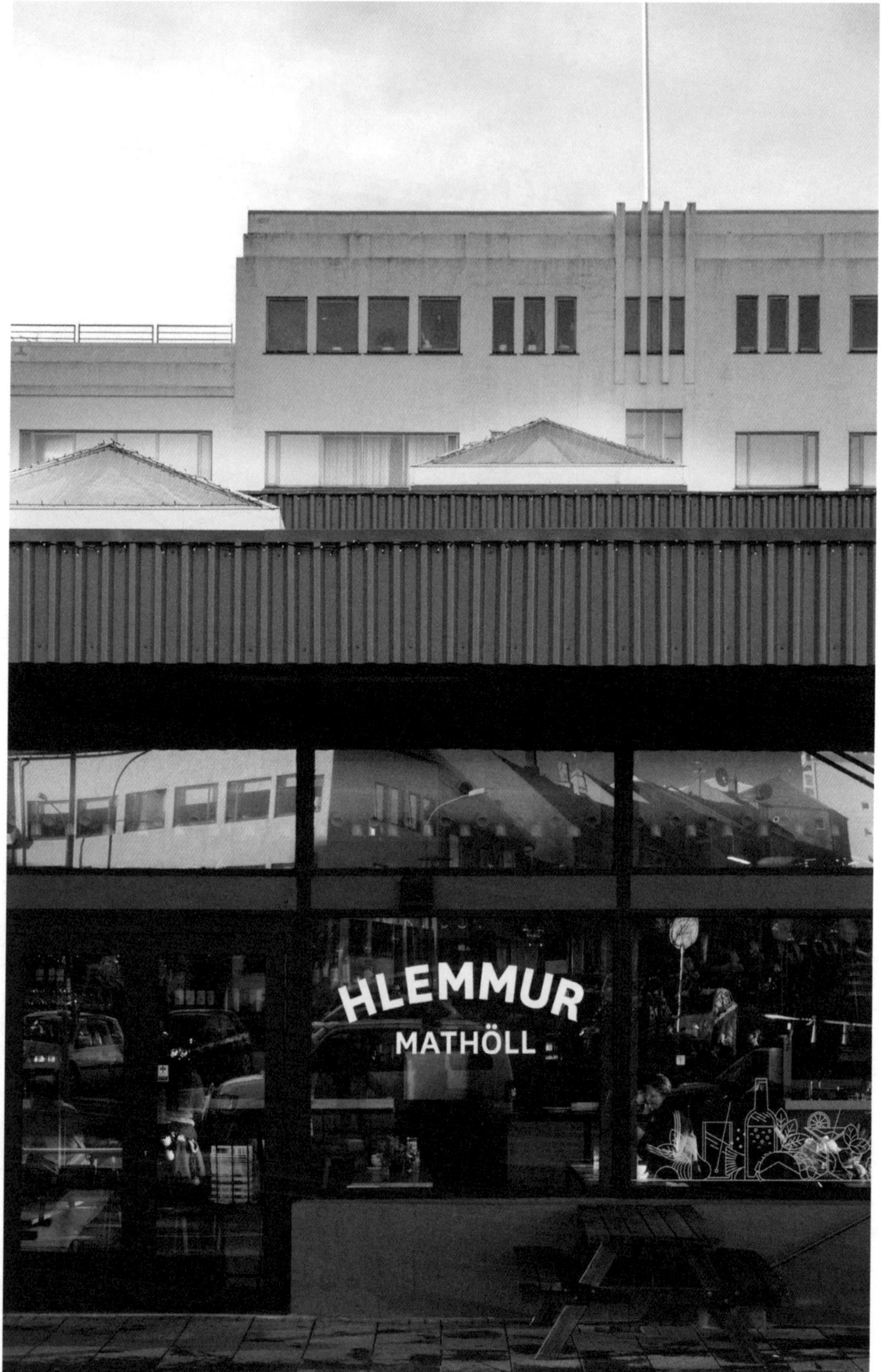
HLEMMUR
MATHÖLL

HLEMMUR MATHÖLL

GOURMET FOOD HALL

"All kinds of food, for all kinds of people" - Hlemmur Mathöll is a gourmet food hall located in one of the city's former main bus stations. Instead of being a place to move onwards from, this reinvented space today invites you to slow down and linger with friends. Opened in 2017, Hlemmur has quickly become popular among locals and is an ideal spot for a spontaneous dinner with friends or to start the night out with a glass of wine, a beer or a long drink. In Hlemmur there are 10 restaurants and bars. From an artisan bakery, to a restaurant with a focus on foraged Icelandic ingredients and to steaks from the grill: there is something for everyone at Hlemmur Mathöll.

Laugavegur 107, 105 Reykjavík
www.hlemmurmatholl.is

MOKKA KAFFI

ESPRESSO AND ART SINCE 1958

Mokka Kaffi is one of Reykjavík's oldest cafés and an Icelandic tradition since 1958. It was the first café to serve espresso, cappuccino and café latte in Iceland. Today Mokka offers a selection of sandwiches and cakes. Those who try Mokka's waffles with cream and jam will be in sweet heaven. The interior has not changed since 1958. Even the sweat marks from patron's jackets are still visible on the wooden walls, making it look like the loyal customers from back then are still sitting on the bench. The decor is Danish-inspired and the art on the walls changes every 4–6 weeks as the café has doubled as an art gallery with new art for sale since it opened.

Skólavörðustígur 3A, 101 Reykjavík
www.mokka.is

EAT

WITH WINE

STAURANT 101 REYKJAV
ESS
RESTAURANT
101
SEN
SIA
REYKJAVIK

ESSENSIA

A TASTE OF ITALY

Vibrant, simple and extraordinary taste: that is Essensia. Located in Hverfisgata, this restaurant brings an Italian twist into the heart of Reykjavík, which includes the interior and furniture. The idea behind Essensia is to bring people together and enjoy high quality cuisine in a casual atmosphere. Quality ingredients and fair prices allow this restaurant to shine, and for this reason people keep coming back. The kitchen holds a specially designed Pavesi oven, a one-of-a-kind hand-turned Berkel cutting knife for ham and sausages and Mareno kitchenware. The Essensia olive oil is home-made by the Schiffini family from Liguria. The wine list is also mostly Italian with the popular house wine coming from Tuscany.

Hverfisgata 4-6, 101 Reykjavík
www.essensia.is

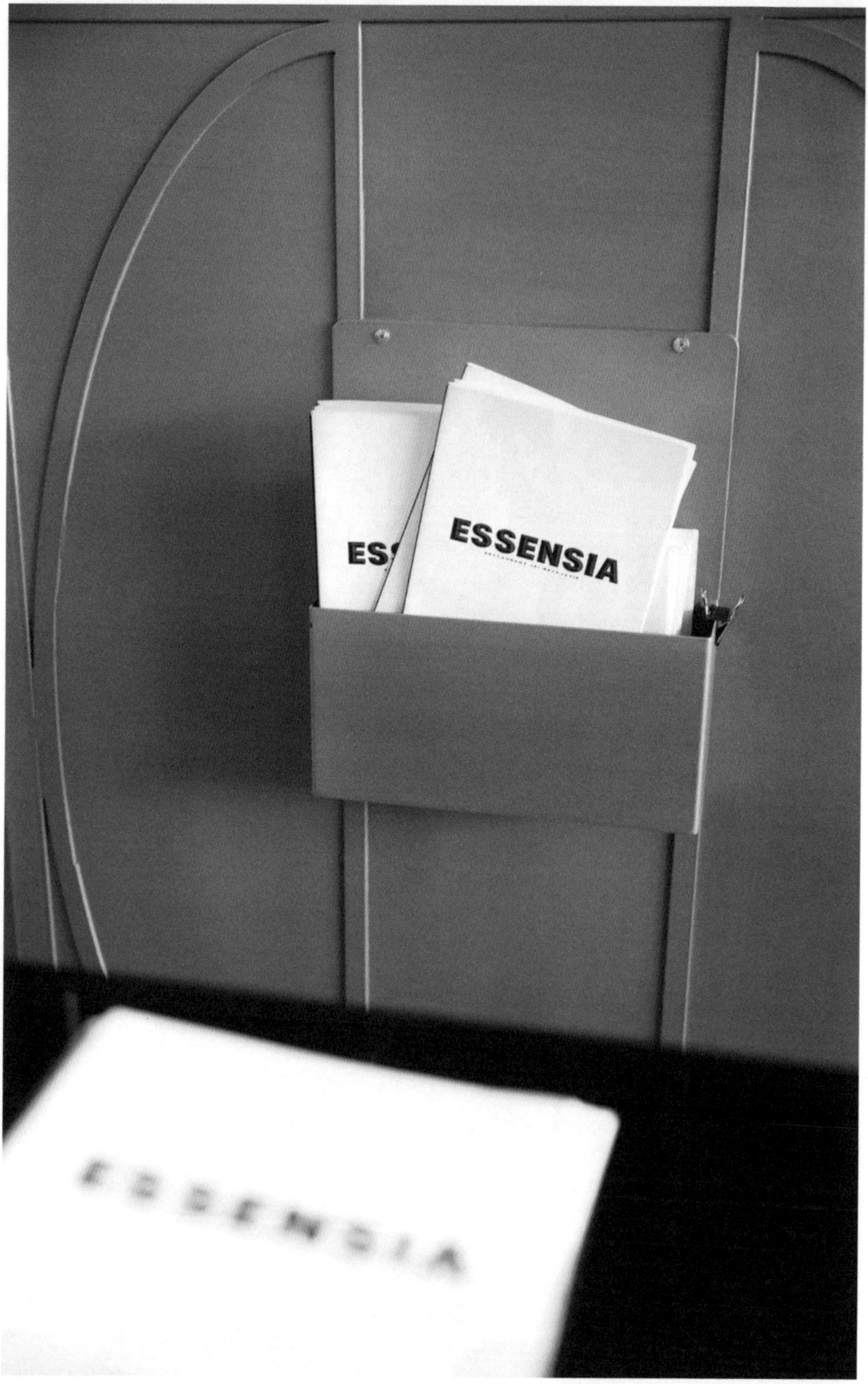
ESSENSIA

MAT BAR

RUN BY PASSIONATE CHEFS

Located at Hverfisgata, this bar is run entirely by its passionate chefs. Mat Bar creates Japanese-Icelandic dishes with an Italian twist, honouring ingredients that are fresh, seasonal and sustainable. Those who are looking for meat will find juicy veal and scrumptious lamb chops, as well as irresistible fish delicacies. The monochrome floor tiles, combined with the brown leather sofa, give substance to a modern stylish interior. Mat Bar is proud of its creativity and Nordic roots. Today, it's a bohemian paradise, oozing with soul – at great prices.

Hverfisgata 26, 101 Reykjavík
www.matbar.is

MATUR OG DRYKKUR
FISKUR DAGSINS
FISH OF THE DAY
- Karfi -
- Red Fish -
Carrots & Garlic purée
Hollandaise sauce
Seaweed
Salted red currant
BEER SPECIALS
THREE COURSE OF THE DAY
CURED ARCTIC CHAR
FISH OF THE DAY
PUMPKINPIE with WHITE CHOCOLATE FOAM
SEASONAL DRAFT
CHERRY SOUR 1450

MATUR OG DRYKKUR

INSPIRING TRADITIONAL ICELANDIC CUISINE

This house was built in 1924 and used as a salt fish factory until the end of the 1960s. Today, Matur og Drykkur is an exquisite seafood restaurant located in the old harbour. Inspired by traditional Icelandic cuisine, this restaurant is famous for its bacalao and comes with its own romantic love story. The owner's Barcelonan husband used to sell Icelandic bacalao in Barcelona, and it was always her dream to open a restaurant. When they discovered that this was the factory that produced the bacalao for Barcelona, they knew that this would have to be the place and Matur og Drykkur was born. This restaurant honours old recipes, resulting in delicious dishes with a creative edge. The à la carte is supplemented by "Icelandic Snacks", along with various tasting menus. All dishes are home-made with first class produce.

Grandagarður 2, 101 Reykjavík
www.maturogdrykkur.is

FLATEY

PIZZA NAPOLETANA

True pizza Napoletana is now a reality in the heart of Reykjavík. Open every day, Flatey became a temple-like institution and has been packed ever since its opening. The interior is modern industrial in a grey-black-green palette with a hint of New York vibe. Focusing on high quality, raw and fresh ingredients sourced from around the world, the cooking time is also vital at Flatey - baked at 500°C in a custom electric oven for less than a minute makes the fresh mozzarella cheese creamy and milky. These four young entrepreneurs are showing that pizza can be more than just basic food. Don't forget to ask about the pizza of the day.

Grandagarður 11, 101 Reykjavík
www.flatey.pizza

nutella
PIZZA
NAPOLETANA

KOPAR

TRUE ICELANDIC FLAVOURS

Surprise and seduction are the keywords at this restaurant. Kopar is influenced by its surroundings: the old harbor, the ships, the pulsating city centre - old meets new, and is cleverly combined. Inside the restaurant one can watch the harbour life, the fishermen and people walking along the lively harbour. The energetic atmosphere of the old port is part of the experience when having lunch or dinner at Kopar. Special features at Kopar are the exciting ingredients and the variety of dishes. Despite her young age, chef Ylfa Helgadóttir has received much attention for her work and numerous awards for her cooking. Ylfa is known for working with Icelandic products and finding unexpected combinations.

Geirsgata 3, 101 Reykjavík
www.koparrestaurant.is

SUMAC GRILL + DRINKS

SEDUCED BY FLAVOURS FROM LEBANON

Combine Moroccan flair, colourful spices, Icelandic seasonal ingredients, edible flowers et voila: an eclectically seductive culinary affair named Sumac is born. Located in downtown Reykjavík and owned by star chef Þráinn Freyr Vigfússon, Sumac brings exotic and flavourful foods to Iceland. Locals as well as visitors spoil their taste buds with flamboyant cocktail mixes and a 7-course meze to share. The orange-coloured interior emphasises the variety, finesse and elegance of this zesty, charming Icelandic restaurant. Þráinn owns another gourmet temple right behind Sumac: ÓX resembles a cosy living room and is Iceland's smallest restaurant. At ÓX, a 12-course menu is exclusively prepared in front of not more than 12 people.

Laugavegur 28, 101 Reykjavík
www.sumac.is

MARSHALL HOUSE

DINING WITH ART

Once a herring factory, today a magnet for creative spaces. Reykjavík's art hub is home to three institutions: The Living Art Museum, Gallery Kling & Bang, and Ólafur Elíasson's only Icelandic studio - a star attraction among locally run art initiatives. Marshall House is located in the harbour district of Grandi, an emerging area where new hotspots regularly pop up. On the ground floor is a chic sit-down restaurant and bar, serving Italian-inspired and fish-dominated dishes. With its high ceilings and huge windows, its concrete floor and steel girders, Marshall House conveys a unique industrial chic harbour atmosphere.

Grandagarður 20, 101 Reykjavík
www.marshallhusid.is

DILL

NEW NORDIC RESTAURANT

The acclaimed Dill restaurant brings Icelandic tradition alive, combining ingredients such as lamb, dairy and fish in a rather unconventional way. The focus is on natural tastes by preserving all ingredients in the same manner as their Nordic ancestors: salting, drying, smoking, pickling or fermenting. And like the seasons, the menu changes too. Dill is Iceland's only Michelin Star restaurant. Besides an intense passion for cooking, Master Chef Kári Þorsteinsson's greatest pleasure is in getting together with family and friends to enjoy food and wine. Located in a former barn, Dill is connected to the popular house on Hverfisgata 12. A private entrance is provided on Ingólfsstræti.

Hverfisgata 12, 101 Reykjavík
www.dillrestaurant.is

SNAPS BISTRO

FRENCH-STYLE BISTRO

Iceland is famous for its creativity and so is Snaps. This venue is a bistro-style restaurant that caters for breakfast, lunch and dinner and also serves as a bar and club. Located in the city centre, Snaps is the perfect place to meet friends, have a glass of wine or beer and enjoy a gourmet snack prepared by chef Stefan Melsted. The most popular dish is the club sandwich with French fries. The interior is inspired by Scandinavian chic with ceiling-to-floor windows allowing light to flood the restaurant. Wooden bar stools match the wooden floor and the mint green head pieces of the sofas match the hanging plants.

Þórsgata 1, 101 Reykjavík
www.snapsbistro.is

SNAPS

SNAPS
OG SAMLOKUR
LAMBAKÓTILETTUR
NAUTALUND 250 gr.
BOEUF
GEITAOSTUR
CREME BRULEE
EPLA TARTE TATIN
TARTE AU CITRON
SÚKKULAÐIKAKA

NOSTRA

SEASONAL TASTING MENUS

Situated near the sea, Nostra is an Icelandic fine dining restaurant with an emphasis on seasonal and sustainable tasting menus using local ingredients. Herbs and spices are grown in the restaurant's own "green room". Star chef, Carl K. Frederiksen, ensures a unique culinary experience, with fresh local produce and ingredients that are prepared with love. The detailed presentation feeds the eyes too. There are up to 8 courses of exquisite dishes to excite every taste bud. Having worked previously in New York and Copenhagen, some of the chef's mouth-watering creations include raw shrimp and cod tartare and lamb belly terrine with cured eggplant. There is no doubt that Nostra is a true passion project.

Laugavegur 59, 101 Reykjavík
www.nostrarestaurant.is

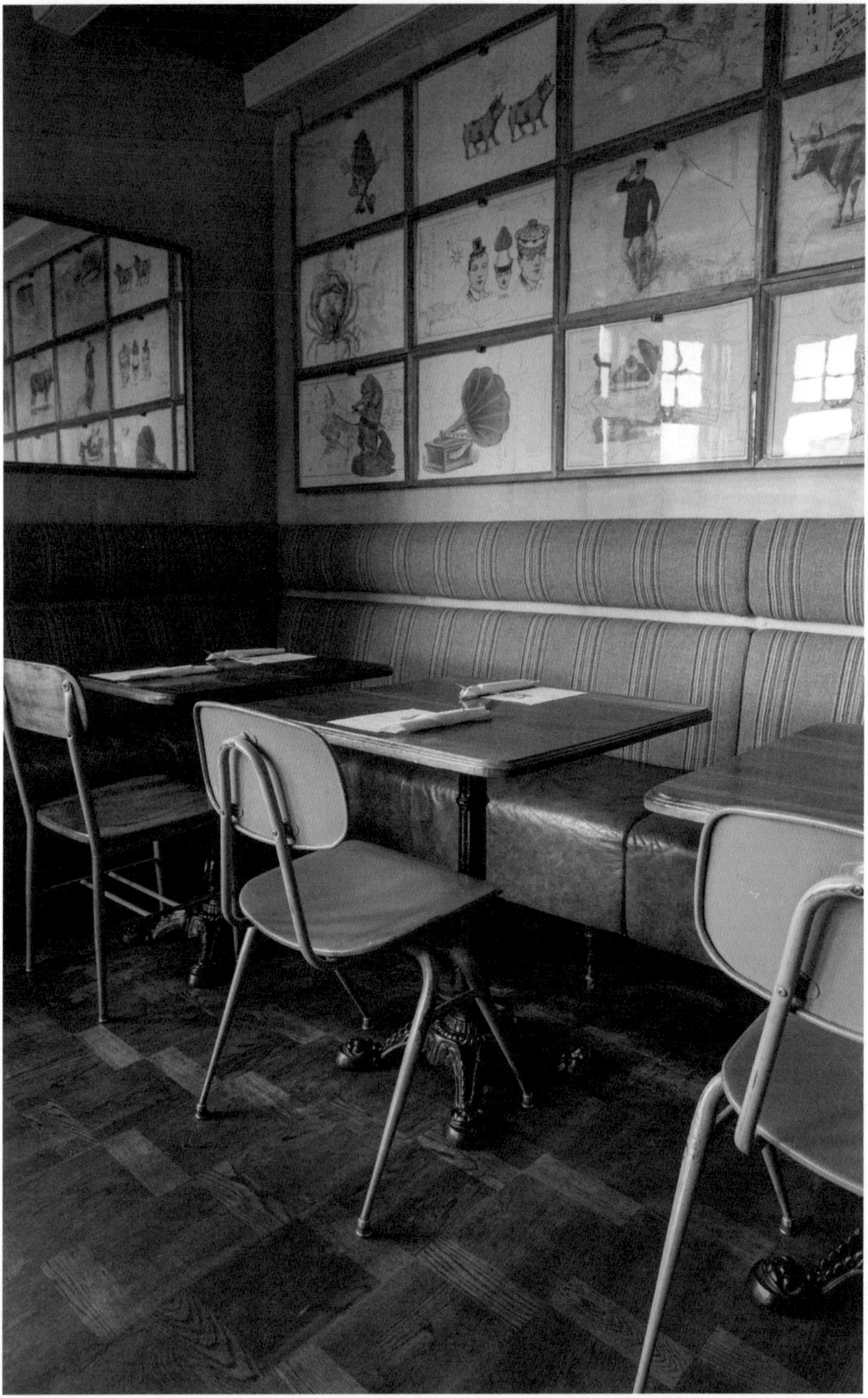

PIZZA PLACE WITH NO NAME

ORDINARY GOURMET PIZZAS

Finding this popular pizzeria can be tricky: there's no sign, but insiders come to Hverfisgata 12, one of Reykjavík's oldest buildings, for gourmet pizzas and fabulous cocktails. It is an eclectic mix of American rustic, old carnival and part museum. The owners are the same as the successful Kex Hostel and award-winning Dill restaurant. Popular beyond the borders of Iceland, the nameless restaurant manages to create a private atmosphere for everyone.

Behind the copper bar, craft beer and other delicious drinks can be ordered. On weekends the pizza place with no name offers a stunning brunch menu.

Hverfisgata 12, 101 Reykjavík
www.hverfisgata12.is

KR.
SMÁRÉTTIR
flur, brenndur ísbúi, blaðlauks mæjó. 1.450 KR.
grænmeti, grasolía. 1.650 KR.

FISKMARKAÐURINN

FINEST FISH

Attention fish and sushi lovers! The Fiskmarkaðurinn fish market is located in an old house with seating area and bar. Indeed, Fiskmarkaðurinn is a restaurant and not a normal fish market. Dramatic presentations of elaborate fish dishes fill the tables, colours and scents of the ocean tickle the senses and the unique sounds of the fishmongers and seamen fill the cold air. Chefs talk shop and find inspiration under this roof where Iceland meets Asia. Which is why this place is renowned for its remarkable sushi bar. Lumpfish roe, chervil, pickled onion, sea truffle and fermented potatoes or rock shrimp tempura served with sweet lemon: this kitchen makes taste buds explode.

Aðalstræti 12, 101 Reykjavík
www.fiskmarkadurinn.is

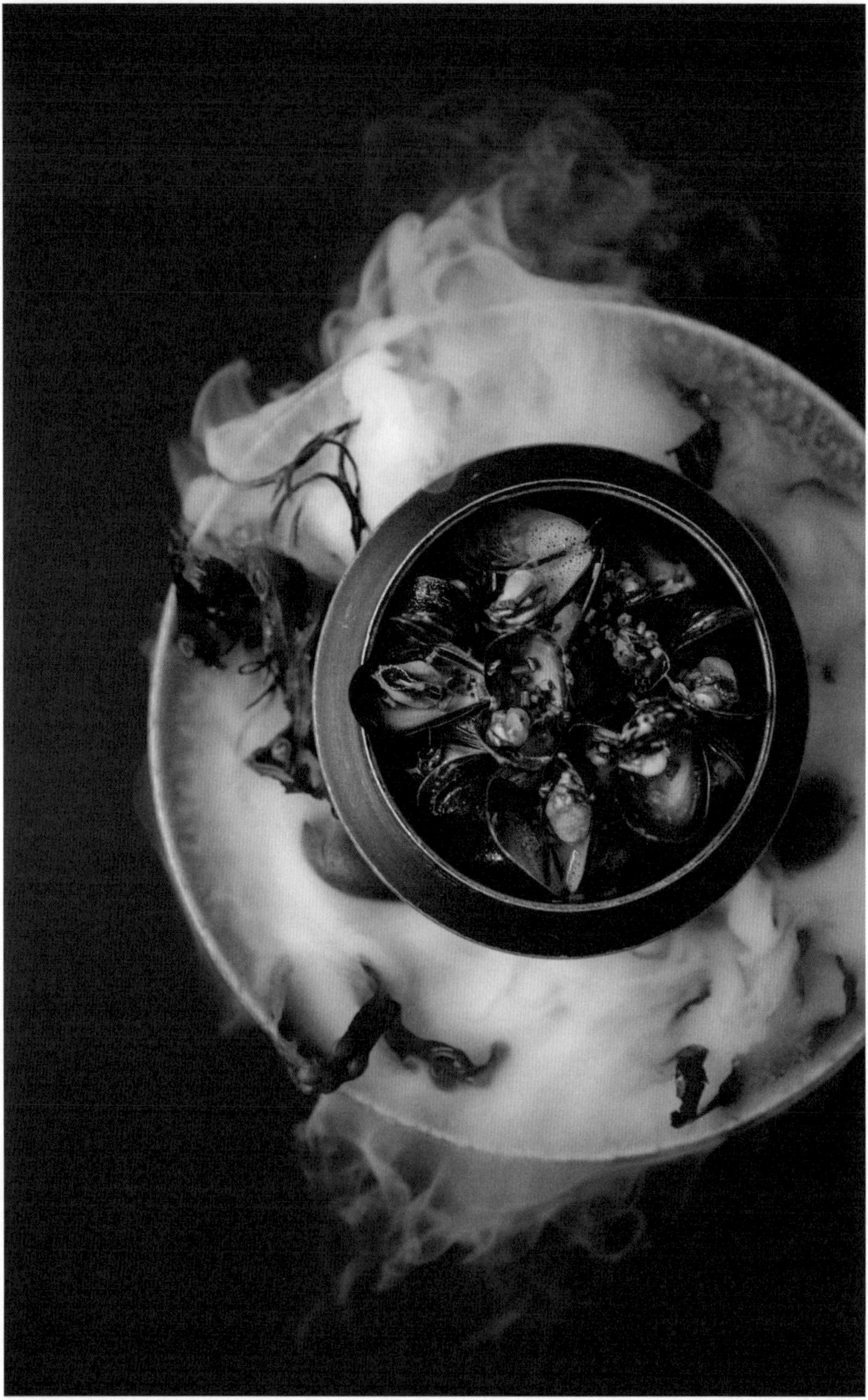

SKELFISKMARKAÐURINN

FRESH SHELLFISH & OYSTERS

One night in Reykjavík and the plate is your oyster. Literally. This seafood palace (Shellfish Market) is brand new and offers space for 150 people in three chic Nordic dining rooms.

Marble floors, marine blue, gold fittings and a wall of illuminated wine bottles make a big impression - and that's before mentioning the food. Skelfiskmarkaðurinn is the first restaurant in Reykjavík focusing solely on fresh shellfish, serving the first ever Icelandic oysters grown in the northern waters of Skjálfandi bay. The atmosphere is cosy and relaxed and the basement of Skelfiskmarkaðurinn can be used as a party room for guests who prefer more privacy.

Klapparstígur 30, 101 Reykjavík
www.skelfiskmarkadurinn.is

DRINK

1 LEON
MALBYGG
2 GUBBI
LAGER LAGER
3
ÖLVERK
RAKIA
5 SÖMMER LÖVIN
6
KEX BREWING\SMIÐJAN
7
8 RVK BREWING
VERUM BARA VINIR
BORG
HUGÓ
9
10
11 THUNDER ALE
ALEFARM
13 LUMON
14 TUMI HUMALL
FOUNDERS
15 DKML
16. GÚRKENGIN COCKTAIL 1600
HAPPY HOUR
TRY ANY
FOUR 2500-
SESSION

SESSION CRAFT BAR

16 WORLD CLASS TAPS

This is a beer lover's paradise. Situated in a top location on Bankastræti, several of Reykjavík's top barmen and beer nerds banded together to open this spacious craft bar. The main feature of the decor are the mint green walls which probably steer focus towards the holy golden beverage. There are 16 brews to try, from tried-and-tested favourites like Mikkeller & Friends to Icelandic micro-breweries, exotic oddities like a piña colada beer and the Santa Rabarbera - a Berliner Weisse combined with Sour. The Session Craft Bar also knows how to combine beer and champagne. Order a glass of Winale and taste the perfect combination of wine and beer.

Bankastræti 14 2nd floor, 101 Reykjavík
www.sessionrvk.is

IPA
NEMA

MIKKELLER & FRIENDS

DANISH MICRO-BREWERY

Located in Reykjavík's famous nameless corner house on Hverfisgata, the brewery Mikkeller & Friends serves fresh beer from 20 taps and holds a selection of over 100 different bottled beers plus a wide selection of organic wines and spirits. The house used to be Reykjavík's first X-ray clinic and the Icelandic Women Shelter but has been redesigned. The interior of Mikkeller & Friends is a colourful mix with rich circus and theatric elements. It is the creation of renowned set designer Hálfdán Pedersen. The nameless gourmet pizzeria, and the critically acclaimed Dill restaurant can also be found in the house.

Hverfisgata 12, 101 Reykjavík
www.mikkeller.dk

BREWDOG

SCOTTISH CRAFT BEER

BrewDog's Scottish founders, Martin and James, were bored of the industrially brewed beers that dominated the UK beer market and decided to brew their own - with great success. In 2007 BrewDog was born and has grown to an empire with over 46 bars worldwide. BrewDog offers over 20 taps of their own craft beer together with other European and international breweries they love. Of course, a selection of local Icelandic craft brews are also on the menu. What sets the Reykjavík bar apart from other BrewDog pubs is its focus on food. From mussels cooked in Elvis Juice, to baked and cooked duck and poached eggs and beetroot salad, BrewDog is a new hangout spot with good food and plenty of beer.

Frakkastígur 8, 101 Reykjavík
www.brewdog.com

PORT 9

BEST SELECTION OF HAND-PICKED WINES

Port 9 is versatile. It makes magic in the morning and it makes magic in the evening - just differently. A breakfast café from 7.00am to 9.30am, this trendy place in Reykjavík's centre serves freshly baked bread, fruits, smoked salmon, granola, yogurt, skyr, brewed coffee, tea and a selection of hot plates from the kitchen.

In the evening Port 9 turns into a wine bar offering a curated selection of international wines. Smaller dishes with a Mediterranean twist are served with a wine pairing. All wines at Port 9 are organic and natural and made with organically grown grapes.

Veghúsarstígur 9, 101 Reykjavík
www.port9.is

BAR MIAMI

EIGHTIES-STYLE COCKTAIL BAR

Iceland's nightlife is notorious and Reykjavík's bar scene is rather more swanky than casual. So is Miami. Miami is an eighties-style cocktail bar located on Hverfisgata. Intensely colourful custom-made furniture is the trademark of this bar together with custom-tailored suits for staff. The bar sells its own furniture and clothing ranges through their website. In the basement a ping-pong table is set up where patrons can play games among the loud colours. Of course, ping-pong gadgets can be purchased through Miami's website, too. The cocktail menu was crafted by mixology veterans, and the wine and champagne list is well-curated.

Hverfisgata 33, 101 Reykjavík
www.miamihverfisgata.com

PABLO DISCOBAR

TROPICAL-THEMED BAR

Iceland's nightlife is like Pablo Discobar, where drinks are good, the crowd is cool and the dance floor is fun. Pablo Discobar is rather quirky, with multi-coloured decor and a tapas bar on the second floor. Often the wallpaper matches one of the highly talented bartenders' shirts or shoes. At Pablo's everyone is allowed to live a little differently. In fact, this bar inspires one to wear excessively vibrant socks. "Big Ass Margarita" or "Choose your Groove" might be suggestions for conversational topics, but these cocktails ensure that every experience in this lively gathering place is one to be remembered.

Veltusund 1, 101 Reykjavík
www.pablodiscobar.is

PETERSEN SVÍTAN

ROOFTOP LOUNGE AND BAR

Kicking off the weekend in Reykjavík starts at Petersen's rooftop bar. Rumour has it that this is the best rooftop bar in Iceland. Located on the third floor of the historic cinema, this bar has a stunning 360° view of the area which is almost overwhelming when the midnight sun still tickles the sky. Then the terrace is fully packed with food being prepared on an outside grill. In winter Petersen's is cozy and offers live music every week. The bartenders know their art, creating and reinventing colourful cocktails as magical as the northern sky. Because alcohol prices are considered high in Iceland, happy hours are rather long; Petersen's is between 4.00pm and 8.00pm.

Ingólfsstræti 2a, 3rd floor, 101 Reykjavík
www.facebook.com/petersensvitan

SHOP

HÚRRA

STREET APPAREL BOUTIQUE

Apparel boutique, Húrra Reykjavík, has created a buzz and excitement around fashion in Iceland. From shoes to jackets for men and women, Húrra has it all. This label is all about practicality. It offers sneakers to walk fast, hoodies to relax in and all sorts of clothing items in between that exult 'Freedom!'. Two stores are located on Hverfisgata. The iconic white-cube building is dedicated to womenswear and female sneakers, while the store for menswear is just a few meters away. With gorgeous interiors and brilliant lighting caressing the clothes – it's almost as if the items on the shelves call out to the wearer.

Hverfisgata 78, 101 Reykjavík
www.hurrareykjavik.is

GEYSIR

GEYSIR

INSPIRED BY NORDIC CITY LIFE

Geysir designs clothing from its studio in Reykjavík with emphasis on applying Icelandic knitwear tradition to contemporary design. Inspired by life in a Nordic City the core idea behind Geysir is to create timeless everyday clothing for both men and women but with character: long lasting pieces suited for urban lifestyle in a cool climate.
The materials are both locally sourced and mixed with quality textiles from around the world. With several stand-alone stores throughout Iceland, Geysir's flagship stores are located on Skólavörðustígur, one of Reykjavík's most enchanting streets. Geysir Heima is the newest addition to the brand and is also located on Skólavörðustígur.

Skólavörðustígur 16, 101 Reykjavík
www.geysir.com

HAF CONCEPT SPACE

CREATIVELY DRIVEN CONCEPT SPACE

HAF STORE is Reykjavík's boutique for designer products, household items and flowers. Beautiful custom made design products created by excellent Icelandic designers can be purchased here. Hafsteinn Júlíusson and Karitas Sveinsdóttir of HAF STUDIO completely renovated this abandoned harbour side building in their own style. HAF STORE is located on the ground floor with carefully curated product selection where beautiful and meticulously designed products like candles, vases, mats, sweets, books, local art and so much more can be purchased.

HAF STUDIO is on the upper level and there clients can order custom designed furniture. The studio also takes on challenging projects ranging from interior, product, furniture, packaging and experience design.

Geirsgata 7, 101 Reykjavík
www.hafstore.is

PECFD
EDFCZP
FELOPZD
DEFPOTEC

MYCONCEPTSTORE

ICELANDIC DESIGN PRODUCTS

Located in the heart of Reykjavík, this store makes designer's hearts beat faster. High-end stylish collectables, including leather goods, jewellery, wooden watches and clothing are available. Even vintage postcards and photographs can be bought here. Myconceptstore has also established an organic skincare range following its mission to offer beautiful things that are hard to find elsewhere. The core element of all products at Myconceptstore is Icelandic design: minimalism and clean compositions inspired by local culture and the country's unique natural landscapes. Eco-consciousness also plays a fundamental role in Icelandic design, as is manifested in the recycling and repurposing of objects as well as the utilization of remnant materials.

Laugavegur 45, 101 Reykjavík
www.myconceptstore.is

ARN

VARMA

THE WARMTH OF ICELAND

Sweaters, socks, cardigans, blankets and scarfs - Varma is the warmth of Iceland. This company produces knitwear made in Reykjavík. The wool is warm, light and breathable and comes from local sheep. Varma honours Iceland's history and shows respect to Mother Earth using and producing wool that is sustainable and environmentally friendly. The wool is processed in its country of origin and the cleaning of the wool involves natural water and geothermal energy. The sheep roam freely and graze wild flora. To keep sheep, nature and customers happy, Varma uses no chemicals or detergents. Varma makes every effort to improve the texture and softness of the wool without losing its inherent qualities.

www.varma.is

BJARNI SIGURÐSSON

ICELANDIC CERAMIC ARTIST

In 1996 Bjarni gave up his career as a banker to dedicate himself to his passion: ceramics. His work is inspired by the constantly evolving Icelandic landscape - from the rough textures of the glacier lagoon, Jökulsarlon, or the gentle basalt steps of Vik Beach. His glazes are unique, giving his work an elegant, yet intimate touch. Bjarni's ceramics are found all over the world and have attracted much attention in the US market - they can be found, for example, at the US household chain ABC Carpet and Home. In Reykjavík, his works can be found at the gallery Stígur, which he runs together with other artists. It is not easy to decide which piece of ceramic to buy: each piece radiates its own character and, above all, the love and care with which it was prepared.

Skólavörðustígur 17, 101 Reykjavík
www.bjarni.co

FARMERS MARKET

FARMERS & FRIENDS

MODERN ICELANDIC FASHION BRAND

Farmers Market is one of Iceland's iconic fashion and design companies, combining modernity with classic Icelandic heritage. Great value is placed on natural materials such as wool and cotton, muted colours and craftsmanship, and all items are suitable for Icelandic city life. These chic Nordic items, including accessories and books, can be purchased at the Farmers Market's flagship store, Farmers & Friends. It is situated in the old harbour district, just 20 minutes from the city centre. Founded in 2005, Farmers Market has become a staple in Icelandic fashion, found in the closets of artists, musicians, everyday Icelanders and hip tourists.

Hólmaslóð 2, 101 Reykjavík
www.farmersmarket.is

KINFOLK
NÍNA S.

GEYSIR HEIMA

GREAT RANGE OF HOME DECOR

If one enters this store the chances of leaving with a beloved new item for your home are high. Geysir Heima is an upscale homeware store and the latest addition to Geysir's clothing stores - conveniently located just across the road. The word "heima" means "home" in Icelandic and perfectly describes what this store is all about. Geysir Heima sells a carefully selected range of home decor and design goods from various brands, including Andrée Jardin, Angan Skincare, Atelier Dottir, Bloc Studios, Hasami Porcelain, Kaas + Heger, Korkimon, La Petite Papeterie Française, Minimum Design, WDLND, Yield and Ystudio. In the basement, there is also an art gallery that regularly exhibits the work of local artists and designers.

Skólavörðustígur 12, 101 Reykjavík
www.geysir.com

KORMÁKUR & SKJÖLDUR

INSPIRED BY BRITISH FASHION

Kormákur & Skjöldur brings a timeless elegance to men's fashion. Reykjavík is home to a diverse variety of local fashion brands, many of whom have their own downtown stores and boutiques. This gentleman's fashion label is the king of Reykjavík's menswear stores. A variety of shirts, accessories and suits in classic cuts can be found from throughout the decades. All items are made from high-end material and tailored to fit. Kormákur & Skjöldur is inspired by British fashion, focusing on wool garments to beat the Nordic ice in style. Items are priced accordingly, but are worth it - their clothing is of the highest quality.

Laugavegi 59, 101 Reykjavík
www.herrafataverslun.is

FISCHER

A PLACE FOR ALL SENSES

Concept store and art space, Fischer cares about the human body and soul. The store's founding siblings and their boyfriends practice mindfulness to create visually attractive and healthy products for all senses: rosa candles with recycled soy wax, Icelandic medicinal oils or charcoal toothpaste and deodorant, perfume, music or plant-shaped lighting. Everything in the shop represents the magic of Iceland and the healing property of nature's plants. No-nonsense ingredients are a core value at Fischer. This store is a place where people can rest in their senses. Its mission is to fulfil and convey visual beauty, synthesising and harmonising with the human senses.

Fischersund, 101 Reykjavík
www.fischersund.com

NORDIC
EMBRACE
KARHU

AKKÚRAT

HANDPICKED DESIGN PRODUCTS

Reykjavík still offers a wide range of individual choices for those who prefer an exclusive experience. Located in the historic part of Iceland's capital, Akkúrat is the place to go for eco-friendly, ethical clothing and homeware. This concept store offers the best of Nordic design. Handpicked products such as fisherman sweaters, wallpaper collages, bags or hand painted mugs from extravagant designers and artists from Iceland and from neighbouring Nordic countries can be purchased. Supported by the Iceland Design Centre, this concept store comes with its own venue to create a living space for events and exhibitions. Akkúrat collaborates with designers and artists in a space where people meet others and become inspired.

Aðalstræti 2, 101 Reykjavík
www.akkurat.is

KVARTÝRA №49

CONCEPT STORE IN REYKJAVÍK

Icelanders are known for being extremely sociable, maybe that is why their inspiration comes from community and culture with a strong focus on family life and caring for children. Being social is also the central aspect of the concept store Kvartyra49, located in Reykjavík's city centre. Fashion victims find quality clothing from around the world - on display and for sale - along with authentic jewellery and carefully selected albums and magazines. Delicious coffee is available while chatting to friends or trying on new items. Kvartyra49 is the place to get to know the Icelandic art scene.

Laugavegur 49, 101 Reykjavík
www.kvartyra49.is

EXPLORE

Iceland's unique landscape is filled with equally spectacular architecture. Characterised by Scandinavian design, it has adapted Iceland's dramatic landscapes and traditions.
In the "explore" category you'll find personally selected design-wise hotels, art museums, and cultural sights to inspire your stay.

HARPA

CONCERT HALL AND CONFERENCE CENTRE

Reykjavík's icon is the Harpa concert hall. It is Iceland's greatest and most distinguished landmark and a cultural and social centre in the heart of the city. Harpa offers outstanding facilities for events, whether they be concerts, conferences, exhibitions, meetings or other cultural events. The concert hall has also received other awards, not only for great performances and concerts, and Harpa's grand-scale, award-winning architecture has attracted 4 million guests since its opening in May 2011. This cultural centre in Iceland stands out as a large, radiant sculpture, reflecting both sky and harbour as well as the vibrant life of the city. The spectacular facades were designed by international architects. The halls form a mountain-like wall when seen from the foyer.

Austurbakki 2, 101 Reykjavík
www.harpa.is

REYKJAVÍK ART MUSEUM

LEADING ART MUSEUM IN ICELAND

Located in the oldest part of Reykjavík, once an old harbour warehouse and now a modern soaring steel-and-concrete exhibition space, Hafnarhús represents local and international contemporary artists in six galleries. The building was erected in the 1930s and at the time it was one of the largest buildings in the country. Today the museum exhibits contemporary Icelandic art, video installations, paintings and sculptures. Hafnarhús is also home to the comic-book-style paintings of Iceland's political artist Erró (1932), a significant player in the international pop art scene. The building was renovated by Studio Grandi architects in 1998-2000 to house the Reykjavík Art Museum.

Tryggvagata 17, 101 Reykjavík
www.artmuseum.is

HALLGRÍMSKIRKJA

INSPIRED BY ICELANDIC TRADITIONS

One thing always stands out in Reykjavík: the tower of the Hallgrímskirkja, a Protestant-Lutheran parish church in the city centre. It's the largest church in Iceland and the second highest building in the country, and was designed by the state architect Guðjón Samúelsson. The outward appearance is dominated by the Expressionist style, similar to the Grundtvigskirche in Copenhagen. The white colour is reminiscent of the glaciers. The very bright interior of the church is achieved by extensive stained glass windows and, unusually, behind the main altar you can see sky and clouds through additional windows. Worth a visit is the tower, from where you have a wide view over the city from above.

Skólavörðuholti, 101 Reykjavík
www.hallgrimskirkja.is

THE RETREAT AT BLUE LAGOON ICELAND

LUXURY SPA BREAK

A trip to the steamy waters of the Blue Lagoon is now even better: carved into an 800-year-old lava field and surrounded by mineral-rich, geothermal seawater, this new luxury hotel seamlessly folds itself into Iceland's landscape. All suites have the same style, with wooden panelling and floor-to-ceiling windows with views onto the lagoon and the moss-covered lava rocks. The two-room Lagoon Suite even has a terrace with direct access to a private lagoon. The interior design reflects the slate grey of the rocks and the earthy tones of the moss outside. Staying at this hotel is an exceptional experience. The extraordinary powers of the geothermal water, the beauty of the volcanic surroundings, and the luxuries of world-class service leave one revived, restored and feeling healthy.

Nordurljosavegur 11, 240 Grindavík
www.bluelagoon.com/accommodation/retreat-hotel

ION ADVENTURE HOTEL

ECO-CONSCIOUS LUXURY

Once an abandoned house in the middle of the Icelandic nowhere, ION is now a boutique hotel surrounded by lush green moss and lava landscape close to the Þingvellir National Park. ION Adventure Hotel offers an unforgettable experience. Whether one is seeking a quiet, soulful soak beneath the Northern Lights, a challenging hike across an ancient glacier, one experiences Hot and Cold, Fire and Ice. Comfortable high-end rooms, a slick restaurant and bar and, of course, an outdoor hot tub spoil every guest and trigger maximum relaxation in a luxurious environment. The hotel interior feels industrial yet warm and welcoming, referencing the natural surroundings through wooden floors, water-saving shower systems and furnishings fashioned from recycled materials.

Nesjavellir, 801 Selfoss
www.ioniceland.is

DEPLAR FARM

REMOTE LUXURY HOTEL

It doesn't get more off-grid than at the luxury Deplar Farm, nestled on the mountainous Troll Peninsula. Icy fairy tales come true at this gateway to wintery outdoor adventures. Whether skiing, kayaking or whale watching in the surrounding fjords, Deplar is the perfect location to view the Aurora Borealis due to the absence of artificial lights. Typically Icelandic, the lodge is made of black timber and the floor-to-ceiling windows allow perfect views into the magical sky. Wellness lovers also find themselves in paradise, hopping from the geothermally-heated indoor/outdoor pool to the flotation tanks and the Viking sauna. Deplar Farm offers 13 en-suite bedrooms with modern and stylish amenities.

570 Fljót, Ólafsfjörður
www.elevenexperience.com

THE BLACK HOUSE

MIXTURE OF MODERN AND OLD STYLE

Once an idea, now a luxury holiday home. Kristinn and Rut have always believed that dreams do come true. Black House is a traditional black timber house common in Iceland in the 18th and 19th centuries. Located in the woods of Hafnarskógur, the fully furnished and traditionally decorated Black House offers pure relaxation. Birds soar in the sky and the Northern Lights are often seen between October and March. The foot of Mount Hafnarfjall, surrounded by Icelandic birch trees, is easily reached, and experienced climbers can walk up within 3 hours. Nature lovers can unwind, breathe fresh air and become one with mother earth to discover and strengthen their true heart's desire.

311 Borgarnes, West-Iceland
www.husrum.is

THE BARN HOUSE

UNIQUE MODERN HOLIDAY HOUSE

Kristinn and Rut have done it again. The fully equipped and modern Barn House is nestled on the shore of the small town Stokkseyri (450 inhabitants). Here, guests find elements from an old ship, and maybe that is why whales and seals are regular visitors to the shore. While relaxing in the living room, it is possible to spot Iceland's most active volcano through the window – Mount Hekla. The last eruption was in 2000. The other volcano one can see from the window is the famous Eyjafjallajökull, which had an enormous eruption in 2010. Besides having a geothermal swimming pool with hot tubs a few meters away and lots of opportunities to watch birds, the Barn House is a great location to see the Northern Lights.

825 Stokkseyri, South-West Iceland
www.husrum.is

COPYRIGHT

. . .

. . .

The publisher would like to thank the following for their kind permission to reproduce their photographs:

Jonathan Gallegos p.10; Skuggi Hotel p.18-21; Exeter Hotel p.22-25, 58, 61; Sand Hotel p.34-37; Apotek Hotel p.38-41; Íris Ann p.66; Marshall House p.110-113; Bar Miami p.148; Geysir Women p.158; Sascha Berner p.184; The Retreat at Blue Lagoon Iceland p.190-195; Deplar Farm p.202-206; Gunnar Sverrisson p.208-215.